This copy of

A Book of Mice

belongs to

A.M.Harvey.

Also available in the series

A Book of Bears
A Book of Pig Tales
A Book of Elephants
A Book of Cats
A Book of Dragons

A BOOK OF MICE

Compiled by Rosemary Debnam

Illustrated by David McKee

BEAVER BOOKS

A Beaver Book
Published by Arrow Books Limited
62 5 Chandos Place, London WC2N 4NW

An imprint of Century Hutchinson Ltd

London Melbourne Sydney Auckland
Johannesburg and agencies throughout the world

First published by William Heinemann 1987

Beaver edition 1988

Typography and general arrangement © William Heinemann Ltd 1987

Illustrations © David McKee 1987 and 1988

This book is sold subject to the condition that it shall not, by way of trade or otherwise, be lent, resold, hired out, or otherwise circulated without the publisher's prior consent in any form of binding or cover other than that in which it is published and without a similar condition including this condition being imposed on the subsequent purchaser.

Set in Janson
by WBC Bristol and Maesteg

Made and printed in Great Britain
by The Guernsey Press Co. Ltd.,
Guernsey, C.I.

ISBN 0 09 956830 6

Contents

The Lion and the Mouse	7
The Town Mouse and the Country Mouse	10
The Original and Vastly Superior Song of Three Blind Mice	15
The Queen of the Field-mice	20
The Emperor's Mouse	30
Mice	33
I am the Magical Mouse	34
The Crow and the Cat	35
House-Mouse	44
Diddle, diddle dumpling, My Son John	50
Pussy at the Mouse's Door	51
Managing without the Moon	52
Kenny	72
The Dormouse and the Doctor	74
I Saw a Ship a-Sailing	79

The publishers are grateful to the following for permission to use copyright material in the English edition of this book: The Bodley Head for *The Town Mouse and The Country Mouse* from Norah Montgomerie's TO READ AND TO TELL: Methuen Children's Books for *The Emperor's Mouse* from TIME AND AGAIN STORIES by Donald Bisset; The Society of Authors as the literary representative of the estate of Rose Fyleman for *Mice* by Rose Fyleman; Victor Gollancz for *The Crow and the Cat* from MRS FRISBY AND THE RATS OF NIMH by R. C. O'Brien; Ursula Moray Williams for *House Mouse* © 1986 Ursula Moray Williams; William Heinemann and the Alison Uttley Literary Property Trust for *Pussy at the Mouses's Door* from TALES OF THE LITTLE BROWN MOUSE by Alison Uttley; Jonathan Cape Ltd for *Managing Without the Moon* from MICE AND MENDELSON © 1986 Joan Aiken and for the Magical Mouse from COLLECTED POEMS by Kenneth Patchen; David McKee for *Kenny* © 1986 David McKee; Methuen Children's Books for *The Dormouse and the Doctor* from WHEN WE WERE VERY YOUNG by A. A. Milne.

Thanks also to Pam Davison and the Sutton Children's Library team for their help in tracing material for this book.

The Lion and the Mouse

A sleeping lion was woken up by a little mouse tickling his face. The lion was angry to be woken up. He had just had a heavy meal and was comfortably sleeping it off. He opened one eye to see who was there. At once the mouse realized he was being watched and ran to safety across the lion's back.

By now the lion was very angry and he turned and pounced on the mouse, catching him between his heavy paws.

'Help, spare me,' cried the mouse, 'and maybe one day I can help you.'

'How could a little scrap like you help the King of the Jungle?' the lion said, and he laughed so much that for a moment he forgot to hold tight and the mouse ran away.

Time went by and one day when the lion was roaming through the jungle, he found himself caught in a net put there by some hunters. He struggled to free himself, but the more he tried the more entangled he became, until at last he roared in anger.

The mouse heard the lion's angry roar and ran to see what was happening. When he saw the lion tied up like a parcel he squeaked with laughter. 'You laughed when I promised I would repay you,' he said, as he began to gnaw through the ropes with his sharp little teeth. 'But now you see, a little mouse *can* help a mighty King.'

Retold from Aesop

The Town Mouse and the Country Mouse

There was once a mouse who lived in the country all by himself. He was very comfortable in his little house, with a larder filled with food.

One day, when it was warm and sunny, he invited his friend, the Town Mouse, to visit him. The Town Mouse said he would be pleased to come, so the Country Mouse lined his house with fresh straw, and collected the best barley, nuts and peas he could find. Then he went to meet his friend.

'You are a lucky fellow,' said the Town Mouse, as they shook hands, 'the country looks beautiful, and the air is so fresh. You've no idea how stuffy it is in town.'

'You must be tired after your long journey,' said the

Country Mouse, as he led his friend into his neat little house. 'Come and sit down. Supper is all ready for you.'

The Town Mouse found the straw hard and prickly, and he looked with disgust at the large pile of nuts and peas his generous host had set out for him. He thought of the creamy cheeses and chocolate cakes he was used to eating, and he picked at a nut here and a pea there, while his friend sat happily nibbling away at some barley.

'What do you do here to amuse yourself?' asked the Town Mouse, who was already feeling restless.

'I go out and gather any food I can find, I potter about until the Owl flies over, and then it's time to go to bed. You see, I've got to get up early before the farmhouse cat is about.'

'What a dull life! How do you put up with it?'

'It may sound dull to you but I'm quite happy.'

'My dear fellow, you don't know what you're missing! Believe me, you're wasting your time in this place. You must come back with me. I'll show you what fun life can be!'

So the Country Mouse agreed to go with his friend to the town.

It was dark when they arrived at the great big house where the Town Mouse lived, but there in the dining-room they found a feast laid out on a long table. The Country Mouse had never seen such rich food before. He stood there staring, his little eyes bright with astonishment. There were cold chicken and hams and a plate of the most delicious cheeses, as well as creamy cakes and sweet biscuits of all shapes and sizes. There were jellies and creams and fruits and nuts, and goodness knows what else.

'Come along, my dear fellow,' said the Town Mouse. 'Just help yourself, and eat as much as you like. There's plenty more where this came from!'

But the Country Mouse nibbled a little of this and a little of that, and couldn't make up his mind what to choose out of so many tasty dishes.

Before he had time to taste anything properly, the door was flung open and in came a crowd of men and women dressed in fine clothes.

The Country Mouse had never seen so many people in one room, and the Town Mouse had to pull him to safety behind a curtain, where he stood shaking with fright.

'We'll stay here till they've gone,' said the Town Mouse, 'then we can finish our supper.'

But before long two pet dogs came running into the room and sniffing all over the floor.

'We'll have to go after all,' said the Town Mouse. 'Follow me.' And they scampered along the skirting board till they came to the mouse-hole. In they ran to the dark dusty place under the floor-boards. And not a moment too soon, for they could hear the pet dogs yapping at the entrance to the mouse-hole.

'Sorry about this, my dear fellow,' said the Town Mouse. 'But don't worry. They'll all go to bed soon and then we'll have peace to eat before the house cat is up and about.'

'I won't stay for that,' said the Country Mouse. 'I've a long journey home so I'll set off at once.'

'You're not going already, are you? Why, you've not seen anything yet – !'

'I have, you know,' said the Country Mouse, 'and it has all been most interesting, and so kind of you to have me. I'll think of you when I'm having a dull time in the country. Good-bye!'

'Good-bye, dear fellow,' said the Town Mouse. 'So sorry you can't stay – !' But the Country Mouse was already out of sight.

Retold from Æsop

The Original and Vastly Superior Song of Three Blind Mice

Three Small Mice
Pined for some fun
They made up their minds to set out and roam;
Said they, ' 'Tis dull to remain at home,'
And all the luggage they took was a comb,
These three Small Mice.

Three Bold Mice
Came to an Inn
'Good evening, Host, can you give us a bed?'
But the Host he grinned and he shook his head;
So they all slept out in a field instead,
These three Bold Mice.

Three Cold Mice
Woke up next morn
They each had a cold and swollen face
Through sleeping all night in an open space;
So they rose quite early and left the place,
These three Cold Mice.

Three Hungry Mice
Searched for some food
But all they found was a walnut shell
That lay by the side of a dried-up well;
Who had eaten the nut they could not tell,
These three Hungry Mice.

Three Starved Mice
Came to a Farm
The Farmer was eating some bread and cheese,
So they all went down on their hands and knees
And squeaked, 'Pray give us a morsel, please,'
These three Starved Mice.

Three Glad Mice
Ate all they could
They felt so happy they danced with glee
But the Farmer's Wife came in to see
What might this merry-making be
Of three Glad Mice.

Three Poor Mice
Soon changed their tune
The Farmer's Wife said, 'What are you at,
And why are you capering round like that?
Just wait a minute: I'll fetch the Cat!'
Oh dear! Poor Mice.

Three Scared Mice
Ran for their lives
They jumped out onto the window ledge,
The mention of 'Cat' set their teeth on edge;
So they hid themselves in the bramble hedge
These three Scared Mice.

Three Sad Mice
What could they do?
The bramble hedge was most unkind:
It scratched their eyes and made them blind
And soon each Mouse went out of his mind,
These three Sad Mice.

Three Blind Mice
See how they run
They all ran after the Farmer's Wife,
Who cut off their tails with a carving knife.
Did you ever see such a thing in your life
As three Blind Mice?

Three Sick Mice
Gave way to tears
They could not see and they had no end;
They sought a Chemist and found a Friend;
He gave them some 'Never Too Late to Mend',
These three Sick Mice.

Three Wise Mice
Rubbed, rubbed away
And soon their tails began to grow,
And their eyes recovered their sight, you know;
They looked in the glass and it told them so,
These three Wise Mice.

Three Proud Mice
Soon settled down
The name of their house I cannot tell;
But they've learnt a trade and are doing well;
If you call upon them, ring the bell
Three times twice.

Anon.

The Queen of the Field-mice

DOROTHY AND her dog Toto are lost. They are looking for the yellow brick road which leads to the Wizard of Oz. Travelling with them are the Scarecrow who wants a brain and the Tin Woodman who wants a heart. The Lion who needs courage is asleep in the poppy field and they cannot wake him. They are all going to ask the Wizard of Oz to help them.

'We cannot be far from the road of yellow brick now,' said the Scarecrow as he stood beside the girl, 'for we have come nearly as far as the river carried us away.'

The Tin Woodman was about to reply when he heard a low growl, and turning his head (which worked beautifully on hinges) he saw a strange beast come bounding over the grass towards them. It was indeed a great yellow wild cat, and the Woodman thought it must be chasing something, for its ears were lying close to its head and its mouth was wide open, showing two rows of ugly teeth, while its red eyes glowed like balls of fire. As it came nearer the Tin Woodman saw that running before the beast was a little grey field-mouse, and although he had no heart he knew it was wrong for the Wild Cat to try to kill such a pretty, harmless creature.

So the Woodman raised his axe, and as the Wild Cat ran by he gave it a quick blow that cut off its head.

The field-mouse, now that it was freed from its enemy, stopped short; and coming slowly up to the Woodman it said in a squeaky little voice: 'Oh, thank you! Thank you for saving my life.'

'Don't speak of it, I beg you,' replied the Woodman. 'I have no heart, you know, so I am careful to help all those who may need a friend, even if it happens to be only a mouse.'

'Only a mouse!' cried the little animal indignantly. 'Why, I am a Queen – the Queen of all the Field-mice!'

'Oh indeed,' said the Woodman, making a bow.

'Therefore you have done a great deed, as well as a brave one, in saving my life,' added the Queen.

At that moment several mice were seen running up as fast as their little legs could carry them, and when they saw their Queen they exclaimed: 'Oh, Your Majesty, we thought you would be killed! How did you manage to escape the great Wild Cat?' And they all bowed so low to the little Queen that they almost stood upon their heads.

'This funny tin man,' she answered, 'killed the Wild Cat and saved my life. So hereafter you must all serve him and obey his slightest wish.'

'We will!' cried all the mice in a shrill chorus. And then they scampered in all directions, for Toto had awakened from his sleep, and seeing all these mice around him he gave one bark of delight and jumped right into the middle of the group. Toto had always loved to chase mice when he lived in Kansas, and he saw no harm in it.

But the Tin Woodman caught the dog in his arms and held him tight, while he called to the mice: 'Come back! Come back! Toto shall not hurt you.'

At this the Queen of the Mice stuck her head out from a clump of grass and asked, in a timid voice: 'Are you sure he will not bite us?'

'I will not let him,' said the Woodman; 'so do not be afraid.'

One by one the mice came creeping back, and Toto did not bark again, although he tried to get out of the Woodman's arms, and would have bitten him had he not known very well he was made of tin. Finally one of the biggest mice spoke.

'Is there anything we can do', it asked, 'to repay you for saving the life of our Queen?'

'Nothing that I know of,' answered the Woodman; but the Scarecrow, who had been trying to think, but could not because his head was stuffed with straw, said quickly:

'Oh yes; you can save our friend the Cowardly Lion, who is asleep in the poppy-bed.'

'A lion!' cried the little Queen. 'Why, he would eat us all up.'

'Oh no,' declared the Scarecrow. 'This lion is a coward.'

'Really?' asked the Mouse.

'He says so himself,' answered the Scarecrow; 'and he would never hurt anyone who is our friend. If you will help us to save him I promise that he shall treat you all with kindness.'

'Very well,' said the Queen, 'we will trust you. But what shall we do?'

'Are there many of these mice which call you Queen and are willing to obey you?'

'Oh yes; there are thousands,' she replied.

'Then send for them all to come here as soon as possible, and let each one bring a long piece of string.'

The Queen turned to the mice that attended her and told them to go at once and get all her people. As soon as they heard her orders they ran away in every direction as fast as possible.

'Now', said the Scarecrow to the Tin Woodman, 'you must go to those trees by the riverside and make a truck that will carry the Lion.'

So the Woodman went at once to the trees and began to work; and he soon made a truck out of the limbs of trees from which he chopped away all the leaves and branches. He fastened it together with wooden pegs and made the four wheels out of short pieces of a big tree-trunk. So fast and so well did he work that by the time the mice began to arrive the truck was all ready for them.

They came from all directions, and there were thousands of them: big mice and little mice and middle-sized mice; and each one brought a piece of string in his mouth. It was about this time that Dorothy woke from her long sleep and opened her eyes.

She was greatly astonished to find herself lying upon the grass, with thousands of mice standing around and looking at her timidly. But the Scarecrow told her about everything and, turning to the dignified little Mouse, he said: 'Permit me to introduce to you Her Majesty, the Queen.'

Dorothy nodded gravely and the Queen made a curtsy, after which she became quite friendly with the little girl.

The Scarecrow and the Woodman now began to fasten the mice to the truck, using the strings they had brought. One end of a string was tied around the neck of each mouse and the other end to the truck. Of course the truck was a thousand times bigger than any of the mice who were to draw it; but when all the mice had been harnessed they were able to pull it quite easily. Even the Scarecrow and the Tin Woodman could sit on it, and were drawn swiftly by their queer little horses to the place where the Lion lay asleep.

After a great deal of hard work (for the Lion was heavy) they managed to get him up on the truck. Then the Queen hurriedly gave her people the order to start, for she feared if the mice stayed among the poppies too long they also would fall asleep.

At first the little creatures, many though they were, could hardly stir the heavily loaded truck; but the Woodman and the Scarecrow both pushed from behind, and they got along better. Soon they rolled the Lion out of the poppy-bed to the green fields, where he could breathe the sweet fresh air again, instead of the poisonous scent of the flowers.

Dorothy came to meet them and thanked the little mice warmly for saving her companion from death.

28

She had grown so fond of the big Lion she was glad he had been rescued.

Then the mice were unharnessed from the truck and scampered away through the grass to their homes. The Queen of the Mice was the last to leave.

'If ever you need us again,' she said, 'come out into the field and call, and we shall hear you and come to your assistance. Goodbye!'

'Goodbye!' they all answered, and away the Queen ran, while Dorothy held Toto tightly lest he should run after her and frighten her.

After this they sat down beside the Lion until he should awaken; and the Scarecrow brought Dorothy some fruit from a tree nearby, which she ate for her dinner.

L. Frank Baum

The Emperor's Mouse

Once upon a time, long, long ago, there lived an Emperor. This Emperor had a little mouse whose name was Misha.

Misha lived in the Emperor's pocket, and sometimes he came out and ran about the room and up the Emperor's sleeve.

One day, when the Emperor was sitting on his throne telling people what to do, a messenger arrived and bowed very low and said, 'Your Majesty! Your mother is coming to tea and she is bringing her cat, Suki, with her.'

'Oh, dear!' said the Emperor. 'Suki is the best mouser

in the whole of the empire. She'll be sure to catch Misha. Whatever shall we do?'

Just then some trumpeters outside blew their trumpets.

'It's your mother,' said the messenger. 'She is here already!'

'Quick!' said the Emperor, 'pass me that thick envelope.'

He got some scissors and cut some holes in it. Then he took a pen and addressed the envelope to himself. At the bottom in big letters he wrote: WITH CARE – DO NOT DROP.

Then, just as his mother and Suki were coming up the path, the Emperor stuck a stamp on the envelope. He put a little bit of cheese inside it. Then he took Misha out of his pocket and put him in the envelope and stuck it down.

'Now hurry out the back way,' he said to the messenger, 'and post this.'

Then the Emperor kissed his mother and said, 'Would you like some tea?'

'Yes, please!' she said. So he gave her some.

Meanwhile Suki was prowling around sniffing everywhere, to see if she could find a mouse to catch. But she couldn't.

Next day, after his mother and Suki had gone home, the postman came to the palace with a letter for the Emperor.

'It's a very wiggly letter, Your Majesty!' said the postman.

The Emperor took it and smiled. 'I *wonder* what's in it?' he said. He opened it – and there was Misha inside, quite safe.

'I *am* glad to see you, Misha,' said the Emperor, holding the mouse in his hand. And then he put him in his pocket.

Donald Bisset

Mice

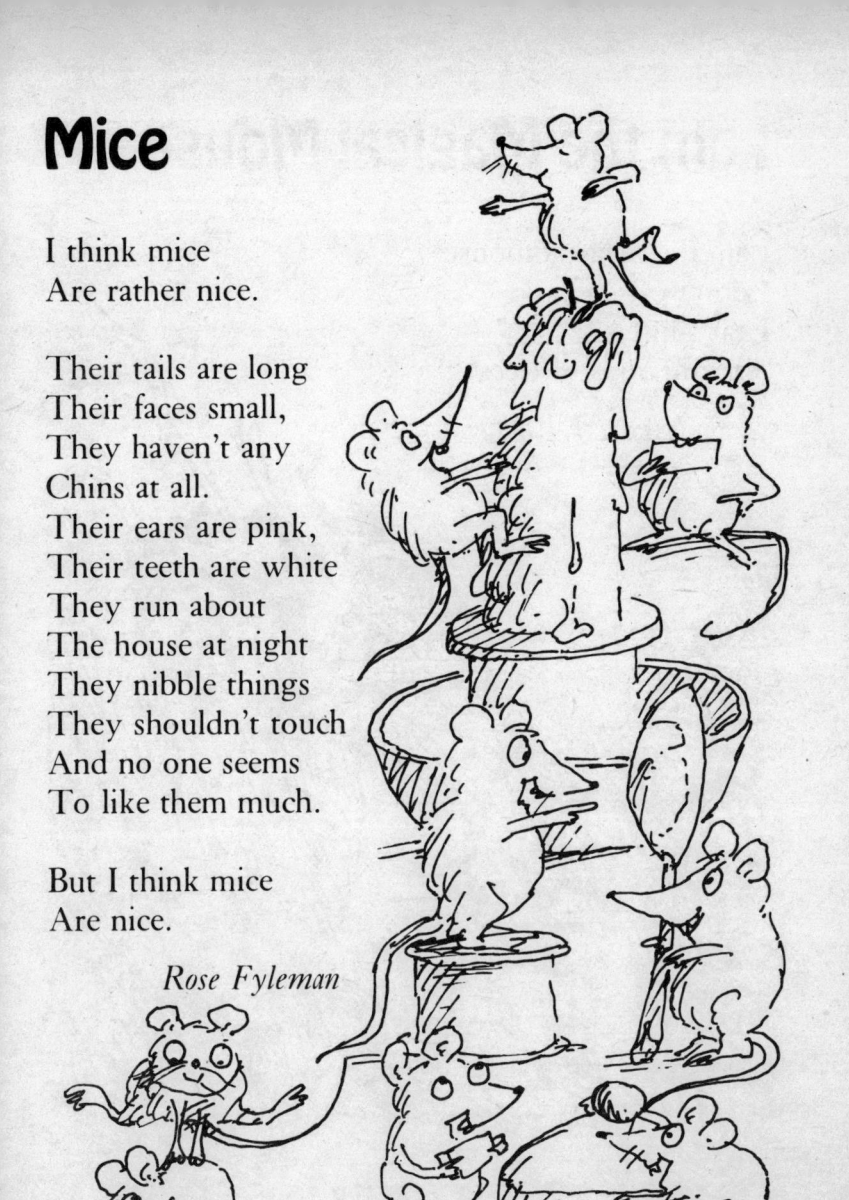

I think mice
Are rather nice.

Their tails are long
Their faces small,
They haven't any
Chins at all.
Their ears are pink,
Their teeth are white
They run about
The house at night
They nibble things
They shouldn't touch
And no one seems
To like them much.

But I think mice
Are nice.

Rose Fyleman

I am the Magical Mouse

I am the magical mouse
I don't eat cheese
I eat sunsets
And the tops of trees

Kenneth Patchen

The Crow and the Cat

Mrs Frisby looked again at the sun and saw that she faced an unpleasant choice. She could go home by the same roundabout way she had come, in which case she would surely end up walking alone in the woods in the dark – a frightening prospect, for at night the forest was alive with danger. Then the owl came out to hunt, and foxes, weasels and strange wild cats stalked among the tree trunks.

The other choice would be dangerous, too, but with luck it would get her home before dark. That would be to take a straighter route, across the farmyard between the barn and the chicken house, going not too close to the house but cutting the distance by half. The cat would be there somewhere, but by daylight – and by staying in the open, away from the shrubs – she could probably spot him before he saw her.

The cat: he was called Dragon. Farmer Fitzgibbon's wife had given him the name as a joke when he was a small kitten pretending to be fierce. But when he grew up, the name turned out to be an apt one. He was enormous, with a huge, broad head and a large mouth full of curving fangs, needle sharp. He had seven claws on each foot and a thick, furry tail, which lashed angrily from side to side. In colour he was orange and white, with glaring yellow eyes; and when he leaped to kill, he gave a high, strangled scream that froze his victims where they stood.

But Mrs Frisby preferred not to think about that. Instead, as she came out of the woods from Mr Ages' house and reached the farmyard fence she thought about Timothy. She thought of how his eyes shone with merriment when he made up small jokes, which he did frequently, and how invariably kind he was to his small, scatterbrained sister Cynthia. The other children sometimes laughed at her when she made mistakes, or grew impatient with her because she was forever losing things, but Timothy never did. Instead, he would help her find them. And when Cynthia herself had been sick in bed with a cold, he had sat by her side for hours and entertained her with stories. He made these up out of his head, and he seemed to have a bottomless supply of them.

Taking a firm grip on her packet of medicine, Mrs Frisby went under the fence and set out towards the farmyard. The first stretch was a long pasture; the barn itself square and red and big, rose in the distance to her right; to her left, farther off were the chicken houses.

When at length she came abreast of the barn, she saw the wire fence that marked the other end of the pasture; and as she approached it, she was startled by a sudden outburst of noise. She thought at first it was a hen, strayed from the chickenyard – caught by a fox? She looked down the fence and saw that it was no hen at all, but a young crow, flapping in the grass, acting most oddly. As she watched, he fluttered to the top wire of the fence, where he perched nervously for a moment. Then he spread his wings, flapped hard, and took off – but after flying four feet he stopped with a snap and crashed to the ground again, shedding a flurry of black feathers and squawking loudly.

He was tied to the fence. A piece of something silvery – it looked like wire – was tangled around one of his legs; the other end of it was caught in the fence. Mrs Frisby walked closer, and then she could see it was not wire after all, but a length of silver-coloured string, probably left over from a Christmas package.

The crow was sitting on the fence, pecking ineffectively at the string with his bill, cawing softly to himself, a miserable sound. After a moment he spread his wings, and she could see he was going to try to fly again.

'Wait,' said Mrs Frisby.

The crow looked down and saw her in the grass.

'Why should I wait? Can't you see I'm caught? I've got to get loose.'

'But if you make so much noise again the cat is sure to hear. If he hasn't heard already.'

'You'd make a noise, too, if you were tied to a fence with a piece of string, and with night coming on.'

'I would not,' said Mrs Frisby, 'if I had any sense and knew there was a cat nearby. Who tied you?' She was trying to calm the crow, who was obviously terrified.

He looked embarrassed and stared at his feet. 'I picked up the string. It got tangled with my foot. I sat on the fence to try to get it off, and it caught on the fence.'

'*Why* did you pick up the string?'

The crow, who was very young indeed – in fact, only a year old – said wearily, 'Because it was shiny.'

'You knew better.'

'I had been told.'

Birdbrain, thought Mrs Frisby, and then recalled what her husband used to say. The size of the brain is no measure of its capacity. And well she might recall it, for the crow's head was double the size of her own.

'Sit quietly,' she said. 'Look towards the house and see if you see the cat.'

'I don't see him. But I can't see behind the bushes. Oh, if I could just fly higher . . .'

'Don't,' said Mrs Frisby. She looked at the sun; it was setting behind the trees. She thought of Timothy, and of the medicine she was carrying. Yet she knew she could not leave the foolish crow there to be killed – and killed he surely would be before sunrise – just for want of a few minutes' work. She might still make it by dusk if she hurried.

'Come down here,' she said. 'I'll get the string off.'

'How?' said the crow dubiously.

'Don't argue. I have only a few minutes.' She said this in a voice so authoritative that the crow fluttered down immediately.

'But if the cat comes . . .' he said.

'If the cat comes, he'll knock you off the fence with one jump and catch you with the next. Be still.' She was already at work with her sharp teeth, gnawing at the string. It was twined and twisted and twined again around his right ankle, and she saw she would have to cut through it three times to get it off.

As she finished the second strand, the crow, who was staring towards the house, suddenly cried out:

'I see the cat!'

'*Quiet!*' whispered Mrs Frisby. 'Does he see us?'

'I don't know. Yes. He's looking at me. I don't think he can see you.'

'Stand perfectly still. Don't get in a panic.' She did not look up but started on the third strand.

'He's moving this way.'

'Fast or slow?'

'Medium. I think he's trying to figure out what I'm doing.'

She cut through the last strand, gave a tug, and the string fell off.

'There, you're free. Fly off, and be quick.'
'But what about you?'
'Maybe he hasn't seen me.'
'But he will. He's coming closer.'

Mrs Frisby looked around. There was not a bit of cover anywhere near, not a rock nor a hole nor a log; nothing at all closer than the chickenyard – and that was in the direction the cat was coming from, and a long way off.

'Look,' said the crow. 'Climb on my back. Quick. And hang on.'

Mrs Frisby did what she was told, first grasping the precious packages of medicine tightly between her teeth.

'Are you on?'
'Yes.'

She gripped the feathers on his back, felt the beat of his powerful black wings, felt a dizzying upward surge, and shut her eyes tight.

'Just in time,' said the crow, and she heard the angry

scream of the cat as he leaped at where they had just been. 'It's lucky you're so light. I can scarcely tell you're there.' Lucky indeed, thought Mrs Frisby; if it had not been for your foolishness I'd never have got into such a scrape. However, she thought it wise not to say so, under the circumstances.

'Where do you live?' asked the crow.

'In the garden patch. Near the big stone.'

'I'll drop you off there.' He banked alarmingly, and for a moment Mrs Frisby thought he meant it literally. But a few seconds later – so fast does the crow fly – they were gliding to earth a yard from her front door.

'Thank you very much,' said Mrs Frisby, hopping to the ground.

'It's I who should be thanking you,' said the crow. 'You saved my life.'

'And you mine.'

'Ah, but that's not quite even. Yours wouldn't have been risked if it had not been for me – and my piece of string.' And since this was just what she had been thinking, Mrs Frisby did not argue.

'We all help one another against the cat,' she said.

'True. Just the same, I am in debt to you. If the time ever comes when I can help you, I hope you will ask me. My name is Jeremy. Mention it to any crow you see in these woods and he will find me.'

'Thank you,' said Mrs Frisby, 'I will remember.'

Jeremy flew away to the woods, and she entered her house, taking the three doses of medicine with her.

Robert C. O'Brien

House-Mouse

Mrs Melody had no children, no friends, no cat, no dog, no parrot or budgerigar. Mrs Melody lived alone.

When people said 'Good-morning' to her, she scowled. When they served her in the shops, she grumbled. When the postman brought her letters, she opened the door the smallest crack to take them in and banged it shut again.

All day long she cleaned her house, wiped the windows, polished the furniture, shone the brasses, and scrubbed the sink. Nobody ever came to see it, which seemed a pity.

Underneath her sink there lived a mouse. He was lonely too. He did no harm in the house. He didn't eat the cheese, he didn't make holes in the wainscot, he didn't leave dirty pawmarks on the shelves. He found all his food out of doors in the garden and only came indoors to get some company.

But Mrs Melody didn't like mice. When she caught sight of him she shouted and yelled as if a tiger had come into the kitchen, enough to frighten any mouse away.

But this mouse did not stay away for long because he was so lonely.

In the houses along the road they had cats, and dogs, and noisy children, and terrible mouse traps. He had very nearly been caught in one. So he came back to Mrs Melody and lived under the sink and tried to keep out of her way.

One day Mrs Melody spent the morning dusting everything in the house, using every one of her four dusters. Afterwards she washed them and hung them out side by side to dry on the clothes line in the garden. Then she emptied out the soapy water, but dropped the soap, and when she stooped to pick it up she slipped and fell headlong, right across the kitchen floor.

She bumped her head on the sink, just where the mouse lived, and out he shot, scared out of his wits, and more scared than ever to find Mrs Melody lying on the floor with her eyes shut.

He ran round and round her. He even tickled her chin with his sharp little nose and whiskers, but nothing would wake her up.

When Mrs Melody did wake up she found she could not move.

'Oh, little mouse! little mouse! If only you were able to help me!' she said. 'If you were a cat you could fetch the neighbours! and if you were a dog you could bark and howl till somebody came. If you were a parrot you could shout: Help! Help! Help! till somebody heard you, but I don't suppose a mouse can do anything at all.'

But a mouse could run just as well as a dog or a cat, and at once he ran across the kitchen and out through a crack underneath the door.

He went out into the garden and looked around. On the clothes line Mrs Melody's dusters were blowing in the wind.

Then the mouse had a great idea.

He ran up the post that held the line and began to nibble at the dusters. He bit and he bit and he bit, dropping little mouthfuls of cotton to the ground till the first duster looked like a big H. Then he attacked the next, and nibbled it into an E. The third duster became an L and the last a P.

HELP hung on the line, secured by clothes pegs and waving in the wind.

The next-door neighbour saw it from her window.

'Something is wrong at Mrs Melody's!' she shouted to the lady in the next house, and the lady passed the message down the street. In a minute everybody was running to Mrs Melody's.

The mouse went indoors and retreated underneath the sink. Soon the doctor arrived and then the ambulance. In less than no time Mrs Melody was whisked away to hospital.

Mrs Melody had broken her leg and it took quite a long time to mend. Everyone was kind to her, and the neighbours brought her sweets and fruit and flowers. Mrs Melody began to smile when she saw them coming, and she also smiled at the nurses and the doctors, and even at the other patients. She became quite a popular old lady in the ward.

'But what we can't understand is how you ever hung that message on the clothes line when your leg was broken!' the neighbours said, 'If we hadn't seen it, you might be lying there now!'

'What message?' asked Mrs Melody.

They brought her the dusters and laid them out on her bed.

H E L P she read.

'It looks almost as if they had been eaten away!' said the neighbours.

'I believe it was my mouse!' said Mrs Melody.

The mouse waited patiently until Mrs Melody came home.

They brought her one day in a taxi, and now all kinds of people came visiting the house.

Mrs Melody was getting on very well indeed.

She had a bright word for all the visitors that came in, and she always introduced them to her mouse.

He felt a little shy now. There was so much unexpected attention. But when the visitors had gone away, and only he and Mrs Melody were left sitting together in the kitchen, he crept out from under the sink and perched on the edge of the grate, washing his whiskers as he listened to her telling him that he was the cleverest mouse in the world, and she meant to keep the dusters for ever to prove it.

Ursula Moray Williams

Diddle, diddle dumpling, My Son John

Diddle, diddle dumpling,
My son John,
Ate a pastry five foot long.
He bit it once, he bit it twice,
And, oh my goodness,
   it was full of mice!

Anon.

Pussy at the Mouse's Door

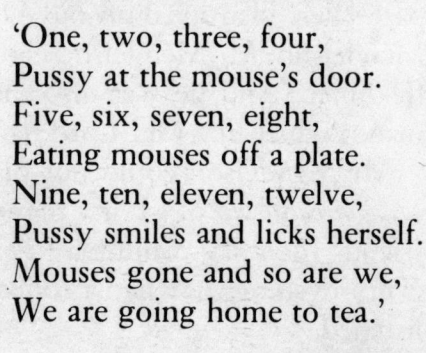

'One, two, three, four,
Pussy at the mouse's door.
Five, six, seven, eight,
Eating mouses off a plate.
Nine, ten, eleven, twelve,
Pussy smiles and licks herself.
Mouses gone and so are we,
We are going home to tea.'

Alison Uttley

Managing without the Moon

All the things I am going to tell you about happened more than a hundred years ago, in a big old park far to the north of England. This park – which was called Midnight Park – belonged to an old lord, who lived in a stable because his house had burned down. And in the park there also lived an old Orkney pony called Mr Mendelson. Mr Mendelson had two friends who were fieldmice. And he was also lucky enough to have a piano, which the Old Lord had given him.

Mr Mendelson could not play the piano himself – who ever heard of a horse playing the piano? – but his friends the mice could play very well indeed, and so every evening they had a concert, and Mr Mendelson listened.

Besides beautiful music, Mr Mendelson was particularly fond of the moon. He loved to watch it when, sometimes, in daytime, it floated across the sky like a white balloon, looking puzzled and lost, as if it were not sure of the way home. And, even better, Mr Mendelson loved the moon at night, when it shone bright as silver and made all the trees in the park throw long shadows across the grass.

Every day Mr Mendelson's two friends the fieldmice Bertha and Gertrude used to spend several hours brushing and combing him all over, pulling the prickles and burrs out of his thick shaggy coat, plaiting his mane, teasing and stroking out his long tail with their tiny clever claws.

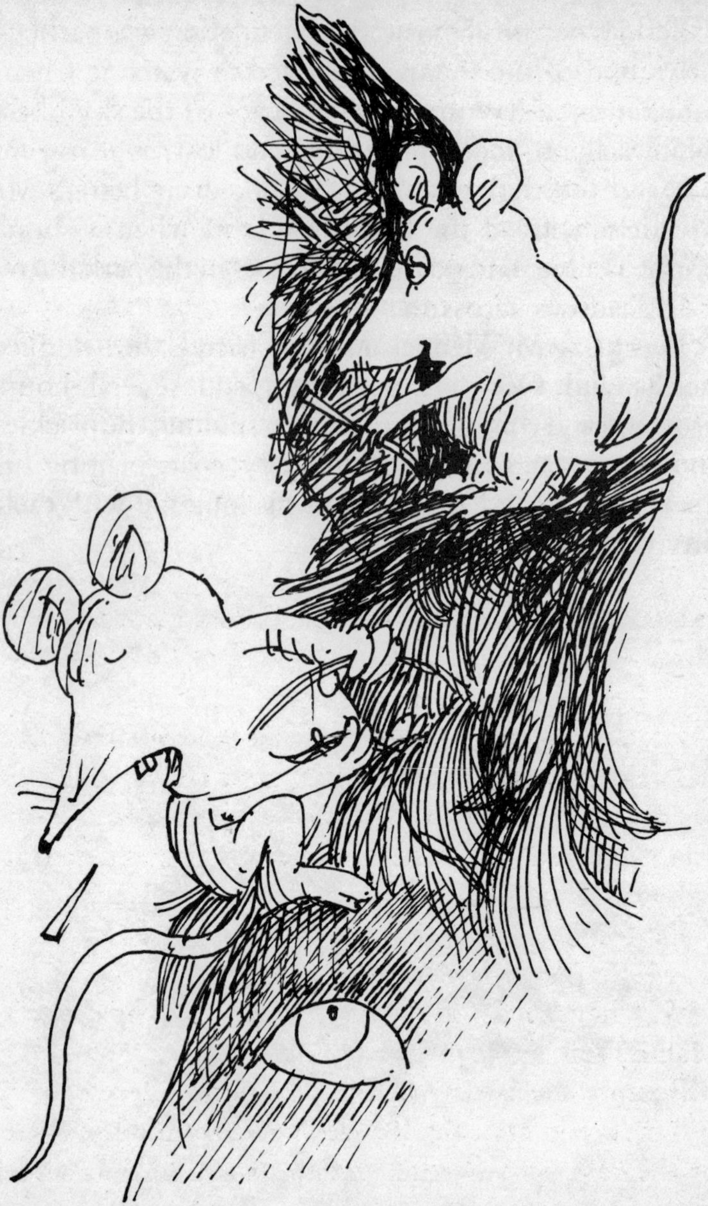

While the two mice tidied up Mr Mendelson they held long argumentative conversations.

The mice were much better informed than Mr Mendelson, because they sometimes went out of the park and under the town, in their tunnels, and they talked to the town mice and heard all the news.

Whereas Mr Mendelson never went anywhere, now that he was so old; sometimes he just stood in one spot for hours together. But he thought a lot, all the time he was standing still.

'So what is the moon?' he asked Bertha one day, when she was brushing out his forelock.

The moon was floating overhead at the time, like a large white soap-bubble.

'The moon?' said Bertha, holding a tuft of forelock between her strong little claws, while she pulled out a thorn with her teeth and spat it away. 'Pffft! Excuse me! The moon's a silver shilling.'

'Excuse *me*!' said Gertrude, who was brushing Mr Mendelson's ears, 'but the moon is *not* a silver shilling. It is a cream cracker. That's why it gets smaller all the time. Somebody is eating it up there. You could not eat a silver shilling.'

'Pardon *me*: it is a shilling.'

'*No*, Bertha. It is a plain biscuit.'

'Whichever it is,' said Mr Mendelson, 'why doesn't it fall down?'

'Because the sky is sticky. Like honey.'

'There you are, Mr Mendelson! Now you're done for the day,' said Bertha, sliding down his tail, while

Gertrude gave a last polish to his shoes. 'Go and look at yourself in the pond.'

There was a tiny round pond in the park where Mr Mendelson lived with the mice. It was not much larger than a round table, and the grass came right to its edge.

Mr Mendelson walked slowly over to the pond and looked into it. There were some red and brown leaves floating about on the water, for autumn had come. Mr Mendelson could see his own reflection looking up at him. His coat was all black and shiny, because the mice had given him such a good brushing.

And then, suddenly, he saw something else in the pond.

'Bertha – Gertrude!' he called anxiously. 'Come here – quick! A bad thing has happened! The moon has fallen into the pond!'

Both mice came scampering to the water's edge and looked in. But now a whole patch of dead leaves had floated across the pond. There was nothing to be seen. The moon's reflection had gone.

'Oh, the moon has sunk down to the bottom, right into the mud!' mourned Mr Mendelson. 'We shall never see it again.'

He looked up at the sky, where clouds were beginning to gather. Sure enough, no moon was there.

'It will float up again,' prophesied Gertrude.

'Biscuits do float, after all.'

'*No*, excuse *me*, Gertrude. It is a shilling, and shillings do *not* float.'

That night it was very cold. Even inside his warm, thick coat, Mr Mendelson felt the cold in his old bones, and shivered in his sleep. Although the cold did not wake him, it made him dream. He dreamed about the gipsy, Dan Sligo, who lived in the woods on the edge of the park, and caught rabbits and cut clothes pegs and stole vegetables from people's gardens. Dan Sligo had a very clever lurcher dog called Jess, who was trained to pick up anything she found and take it back to her master. Jess had been taught to catch fish, too, and could snap a trout from the stream in her jaws without breaking a single one of its scales.

In the old pony's dream he saw Dan Sligo by the pond with a fishing-net; he saw the dog Jess dash into the water and come out with the moon in her teeth and give it to her master. Then the gipsy dropped the moon into his net and slung it over his shoulder and walked away.

'Oy, moy, Dan Sligo has stolen the moon!' mourned

Mr Mendelson in his sleep, and woke himself up. He was so cold, and so worried by his dream, that although it was hardly morning yet, he made his way to the pond, which was some distance from where he had been sleeping with his chin resting on the keyboard of his beloved piano.

The weather was bitterly cold. As Mr Mendelson moved along, his hoofs went scrunch, scrunch, through the grass, which was white with frost.

When Mr Mendelson came close to the pond, what did he see? He saw Dan Sligo, with an axe, very busy,

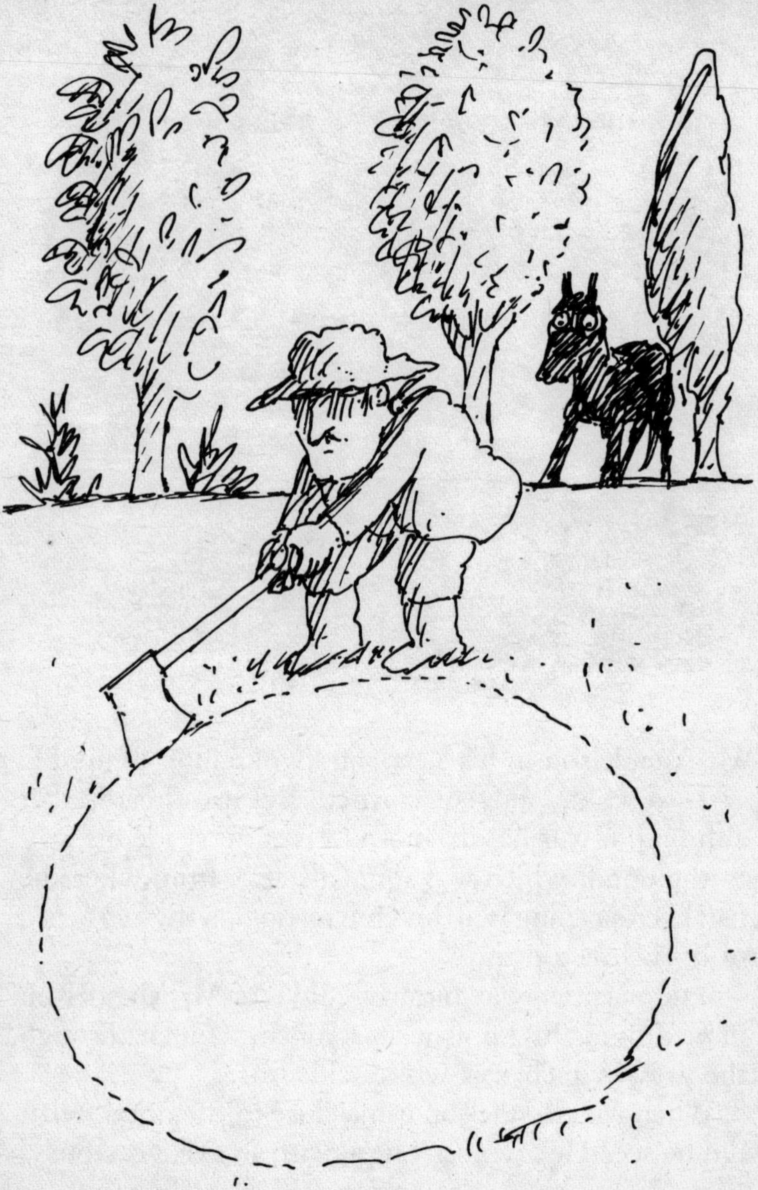

hacking away, all round the rim of the pond. Dan Sligo saw the old pony coming slowly across the white crisp grass.

'How do, Mr Mendelson!' he called cheerfully. 'Up early, ain't 'ee? Don't sleep so good these sharp nights, eh? Ancient bones gets to creaking in the frost, divvn't they? Best ask the Old Lord for a blanket.'

'What are you doing, Dan Sligo?' asked Mr Mendelson. He was very worried at seeing the gipsy working by the pond where the moon lay drowned. His heart went geflip, geflap.

'What am I a-doing?' The gipsy winked. 'Best ask Mr Brown the pastrycook how he makes his ice-cream! A frozen tongue can't tell 'ee no lie, Mr Mendelson!'

And at that, Dan Sligo did an amazing thing. He gave a tilting push to the surface of the pond with his foot. He gave a pull with his arms. And the whole pond seemed to tip sideways in a great white circle. Dan Sligo tipped up the white circle on to its edge, and began to roll it away over the grass.

Mr Mendelson watched him go with starting eyes. 'Stop! Stop! Come back, Dan Sligo!' he called faintly. But the gipsy took no notice. He rolled his round of white over the grass to the park fence where he had a hand-barrow waiting, tipped forward on its wheel. He rolled the white circle straight into the barrow. And then he pushed the barrow away down the hill into the town.

When the two mice arrived, later in the morning, to brush Mr Mendelson's coat, they found the old pony very sad and silent.

'What's the matter, Mr Mendelson?' said Bertha, running up on to his nose, for his head hung down so low that it was an easy jump from a frosty clump of grass. 'Why are you so gloomy?'

'Dan Sligo was here early this morning, and he has stolen the moon out of our pond, and rolled it away down the hill.'

'You're pulling my tail!' gasped Gertrude. 'Stolen the moon? Dan Sligo? Oy, what a scoundrel! Why has he done that?'

'Why ask why? That sneak would steal the egg from his mother's breakfast if he thought he could get it away without her noticing,' said Bertha. 'Of course he'll sell it to somebody. But who would buy the moon?'

'He said something about Mr Brown the pastrycook,' said Mr Mendelson sadly. 'He said, "Ask Mr Brown how he makes his ice-cream." What do you think he meant by that? What *is* ice-cream?'

Even the well-informed mice didn't know that. But they promised Mr Mendelson that they would find out, when they had finished tidying him for the day; they would go and visit their cousins Martha and Charlotte, who lived under Mr Brown's shop and made use of his cake-crumbs.

All day Mr Mendelson wandered sorrowfully about the park. It was a grey cloudy day, very cold. He hardly did more than nibble at the frosty grass. Many, many times he peered sadly into the pond. Often, often, he gazed up at the sky. But no moon was to be seen in either place.

At six o'clock the mice returned and climbed up Mr Mendelson's tail on to the piano, for it was time to play their evening concert. But first, Mr Mendelson was anxious to know what they had found out from their cousins.

'Well? Well? How *does* Mr Brown the pastrycook make his ice-cream?'

'He has a big wooden machine, as big as a barrel, and he turns a handle round and round and round. And then he opens the top and scoops out the ice-cream.'

'Yes? So what is this ice-cream?'

'Charlotte and Martha stole a crumb for us to try. It is round and cold and white, and it melts on your whiskers before you have a chance to taste it,' said Bertha.

'I'm afraid it's quite clear that ice-cream is made from melted moon,' sighed Gertrude.

'Oy, moy!' lamented Mr Mendelson. 'We shall never see our beautiful moon again. Dan Sligo has stolen it and Mr Brown has ground it up and made it into ice-cream.'

The two mice looked at each other and shook their heads.

'For once, Mr Mendelson,' said Bertha, 'I'm afraid you are right.'

They all sat grieving for the moon in silence. Then Gertrude said, 'Well, tears won't fry pancakes. Let's play a bit of music and try to cheer up. Just because the moon is gone, is that a reason to mope?'

'No – you are right,' said her sister. 'We'll have to learn to manage without the moon.'

And without waiting any longer, the two mice began scampering up and down the keyboard of the piano, pressing down the black notes and the white, using their noses, their feet, and even their tails, with terrific dexterity and energy. They made such brilliant and glorious music that the Old Lord, who lived in the stables, heard it, and came rolling himself across the park in his wheelchair to listen and enjoy it at closer quarters.

'Now play the moonlight piece,' said Mr Mendelson, when it was nearly time to stop.

The moonlight piece was his favourite, his particular favourite, for it was slow and thoughtful, moving along at a quiet dreamy pace like the moon gently drifting through the branches of trees, throwing one shadow after another.

As Mr Mendelson listened to it, a tear rolled down each side of his nose. He thought to himself, 'I shall never see the moon again. The nights will always be dark from now on.'

But then – all of a sudden – he noticed that the tears rolling down his nose each had a silvery dot of moon reflected in them. And when he raised his head, there was the moon itself, just climbing out of a hawthorn bush.

'Bertha! Gertrude!' he shouted. 'Look! Look! The moon has come back! Your music must have put it together again!'

All three of them sat gazing in silent amazement as the moon disentangled itself from the bush and moved up into the sky.

Then the Old Lord said, 'Well, well, it's my bedtime. And it's your bedtime too, Mr Mendelson. I brought your blanket tonight. Winter's just around the corner.' And he buckled a warm tartan blanket around the old pony's barrel-stomach, before rolling himself away in his wheelchair.

'What did he mean, winter is just around the corner?' said Gertrude.

'Maybe he meant, just around the cornfield,' suggested Bertha.

'Well anyway,' said Mr Mendelson, 'now we know for certain what the moon is made of. The moon is made of ice-cream. And at least we know, too, that if Dan Sligo should steal it again, you can always get it back with your music.'

So that night Mr Mendelson slept soundly in his blanket, without a single dream. And the mice slept soundly in their mouse-hole, which was warmly lined with combings from Mr Mendelson's thick coat.

Overhead, the moon drifted through the sky, and what it was made of, who can say?

Joan Aiken

KENNY
WHOW! A 20p Coin
I could buy an ice-cream
or I could buy a drink
Heads ice-cream tails a drink
Tails so it's a drink

I could buy a cola
or I could buy an orange
Heads cola Tails Orange
OH NO! I've lost it
I wonder what I'd have done with the change
DRINKS 15p
McKEE

The Dormouse and the Doctor

There once was a Dormouse who lived in a bed
Of delphiniums (blue) and geraniums (red),
And all the day long he'd a wonderful view
Of geraniums (red) and delphiniums (blue).

A Doctor came hurrying round, and he said:
'Tut-tut, I am sorry to find you in bed.
Just say "Ninety-nine," while I look at your chest. . . .
Don't you find that chrysanthemums answer the best?'

The Dormouse looked round at the view and replied
(When he'd said 'Ninety-nine') that he'd tried and
   he'd tried,
And much the most answering things that he knew
Were geraniums (red) and delphiniums (blue).

The Doctor stood frowning and shaking his head,
And he took up his shiny silk hat as he said:
'What the patient requires is a change,' and he went
To see some chrysanthemum people in Kent.

The Dormouse lay there, and he gazed at the view
Of geraniums (red) and delphiniums (blue),
And he knew there was nothing he wanted instead
Of delphiniums (blue) and geraniums (red).

The Doctor came back and, to show what he meant,
He had brought some chrysanthemum cuttings from Kent.
'Now *these*,' he remarked, 'give a *much* better view
Than geraniums (red) and delphiniums (blue).'

They took out their spades and they dug up the bed
Of delphiniums (blue) and geraniums (red),
And they planted chrysanthemums (yellow and white).
'And *now*,' said the Doctor, 'we'll *soon* have you right.'

The Dormouse looked out, and he said with a sigh:
'I suppose all these people know better than I.
It was silly, perhaps, but I *did* like the view
Of geraniums (red) and delphiniums (blue).'

The Doctor came round and examined his chest,
And ordered him Nourishment, Tonics, and Rest.
'How very effective,' he said, as he shook
The thermometer, 'all these chrysanthemums look!'

The Dormouse turned over to shut out the sight
Of the endless chrysanthemums (yellow and white).
'How lovely,' he thought, 'to be back in a bed
Of delphiniums (blue) and geraniums (red).'

The Doctor said, 'Tut! It's another attack!'
And ordered him Milk and Massage-of-the-back,
And Freedom-from-worry and Drives-in-a-car,
And murmured, 'How sweet your chrysanthemums are!'

The Dormouse lay there with his paws to his eyes,
And imagined himself such a pleasant surprise:
'I'll *pretend* the chrysanthemums turn to a bed
Of delphiniums (blue) and geraniums (red)!'

The Doctor next morning was rubbing his hands,
And saying, 'There's nobody quite understands
These cases as I do! The cure has begun!
How fresh the chrysanthemums look in the sun!'

The Dormouse lay happy, his eyes were so tight
He could see no chrysanthemums, yellow or white.
And all that he felt at the back of his head
Were delphiniums (blue) and geraniums (red).

*And that is the reason (Aunt Emily said)
If a Dormouse gets in a chrysanthemum bed,
You will find (so Aunt Emily says) that he lies
Fast asleep on his front with his paws to his eyes.*

A. A. Milne

I Saw a Ship a-Sailing

I saw a ship a-sailing,
A-sailing on the sea;
And Oh! but it was laden
With pretty things for thee.

There were comfits in the cabin,
And apples in the hold,
The sails were made of silk,
And the masts of beaten gold.

The four and twenty sailors
That stood between the decks
Were four and twenty white mice
With chains about their necks.

The Captain was a duck,
With a packet on his back,
And when the ship began to move
The Captain said Quack! Quack!

Anon.